CHASING
LEAVES

THOUGHTS FOR THE DAY

Eddie Askew

By the same author:
A Silence and a Shouting
Disguises of Love
Many Voices One Voice
No Strange Land
Facing the Storm
Breaking the Rules
Cross Purposes
Slower than Butterflies
Music on the Wind
Edge of Daylight (Memoirs)
Talking with Hedgehogs (book and spoken word cassette)
Unexpected Journeys
Love is a Wild Bird (book and spoken word cassette)
Encounters

Published, edited and distributed by
TLM Trading Limited
www.tlmtrading.com

All Bible quotations from the NEW INTERNATIONAL VERSION,
by permission of the International Bible Society.

First published 2005, reprinted 2011

Editorial and Design by Creative Plus Publishing Ltd.
2nd Floor, 151 High Street, Billericay CM12 9AB
www.creative-plus.co.uk

Printed and bound in Singapore by Imago
ISBN 0-902731-59-9

Cover picture (printed in full on pp 24-25): Golden Days, *Watercolour*
Title page: Lilies, *Watercolour*

Dedication

To all at TLM Trading Limited,
staff and volunteers,
for their friendship, hard work and support.
With thanks.

Above:
Dancing Trees, *Gouache*

Foreword

Although I have never had the privilege of meeting Eddie Askew, I have read and appreciated so many of his books that I feel as if I know him! In fact, I have been very grateful that he has allowed me to include some of his prayers and poems in my own anthologies.

In the preface of this, his latest book, he suggests that everyone has the ability to 'stay awake and aware, to tune in and listen'. I suppose this is true to a certain extent, but Eddie seems to have developed this amazing gift to the full – to take an ordinary life situation and bring a spiritual dimension to it. His sense of humour is disarming and the depth of his understanding of humanity, inspirational. His poems are so graphic and the watercolours enhance the atmosphere of the themes in a unique way. I'm sure many of us would love to have them hanging on the walls of our living rooms!

Thank you Eddie, for the blessing that you and your books and broadcasts have been to so many, over so many years.

More than that, thank you for the example your life has been, as an illustration of 'running with endurance, the race that God has set before us'. I salute you, and hope that *Chasing the Leaves* will be your most successful book yet!

Fiona Castle, 2005

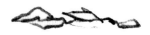

O rdinary humdrum life. Is there any such thing?

Wherever you go, wherever you look, there is interest. Little events that provoke new thoughts; nothing earth-shattering, just small encouragements to share at the day's beginning. Something someone says or does, or a 'happenstance' that catches the imagination. All it takes is the ability to stay awake and aware, to tune in, and listen.

We can all do that.

Eddie Askew, June 2005

Overleaf:
End of Day, *Watercolour*

Luke 10:27

'Love the Lord your God with all your heart and with all your soul
and with all your strength and with all your mind';
and 'Love your neighbour as yourself.'

We acquired Milli, our new puppy, a Cavalier King Charles Spaniel, during the last days of autumn. She loves leaves. In her view, going into the garden has nothing to do with toilet training. It was just a glorious opportunity to fight the leaves as they dropped from the trees. First, she'd sniff at them as they lay quietly in corners but she was really waiting for the wind.

When it came, swirling the leaves, moving them, lifting them, she was ecstatic. Maybe she saw them as barbarian hordes to be attacked and repelled; she would leap and run and pounce on them. Sometimes it was just one particular leaf she'd follow and capture, then chew it to bits. It was fun to watch, although I'm sure there's a serious purpose behind it, an instinctive urge in her to practise and develop her agility and strength.

What impressed me most though, after the laughter, was the way she threw herself into the adventure. It was all or nothing. Fighting the leaves took all her attention, all her energy and commitment. I'm supposed to be training Milli, but I think she's training me. She's telling me that if I want to make a good job of all I do today I'd better use the same commitment and energy she uses. That goes for our friendships too.

And when it's all over, Milli knows just how to curl up and relax – on the sofa. I find that easier to do.

Lord of love and laughter, I give myself
to you without reserve. At least, that's
what I aim to do. Give me a helping hand.

And afterwards, I will pour out my Spirit on all people. Your sons and daughters will prophesy, your old men will dream dreams, your young men will see visions.

I've just got back from a quick trip to Jersey. I flew over to set up an exhibition of my watercolours. The job done, I borrowed a car and drove round the coast to a lovely beach, two miles of clean white sand. Tide lines of seaweed and cockle-shells curved away into the distance. A flock of black and white oyster-catchers watched along the water's edge.

And then I saw the sand castles. Yesterday's sand castles, the sand already dry and crumbling, the sharp outlines eroded, the breeze nibbling at the edges, the surrounding moats filling up. I thought of the castles I'd built as a boy – heaps of sand patted firmly into place with my spade, the hand-shaped walls, and the turrets planted by upending my bucket. I remembered my dreams of imaginary battles repelling the enemy. Somehow, I always seemed to win.

I stood and looked again at yesterday's castles. Built and loved briefly but now abandoned. I thought of all the childhood dreams they represented, the happiness of yesterday in the sunshine.

Don't abandon your dreams. Hold onto them. Dreams are stronger than sand, they can give shape and texture to life, and they can last much longer than a day. Hold onto your dreams, they give us something to live and hope for, something to plan and struggle for.

Lord of the past and the future,
help me to shape today for good
and find my dreams fulfilled in you.

Accept one another, then, just as Christ accepted you,
in order to bring praise to God.

Someone's discovered that ducks in south-east London quack differently from ducks born and bred in Cornwall. Honestly. Ducks have regional accents! The reason seems to be that London ducks become more strident by having to compete with the sounds of heavy traffic and other noise pollution. Cornish ducks quack more gently. It's quieter in Cornwall, except on Bank holidays. But in the end a duck is a duck right down to the last tail feather, however refined its accent. They all have similar needs – for food and water, especially water, a safe nest, and a sense of belonging.

It sets my imagination going a bit though. What would happen if a well-brought-up Cornish duck took a London drake home to meet her parents? What would they say? "Yes, he's a nice enough bird, but I hope you're not going to marry him."

Maybe that suggests something about us human beings. Whatever our background, our accent, or even what language we speak, God made us human, with similar needs, especially the need to belong, to be accepted. Under the skin, or in the ducks' case under the feathers, we're all the same. The little differences just make life a bit more interesting.

> Lord of diversity, I thank you
> for the differences
> that shape our lives.
> And for loving me for what I am.

For whatever is hidden is meant to be disclosed, and whatever is concealed is meant to be brought out into the open.

Why do archaeologists all wear striped woolly jumpers with holes in the elbows, and rarely comb their hair? I suppose that's not true, but that's the way it looks when they appear on the telly. I'm fascinated by those digging-up-the-past programmes. You know, some man with a metal detector starts walking up and down a field until there's a bleep on his machine. He starts to scratch around to see what's there. More often than not it's a battered beer can he digs up, or a bit of rusty wire, but sometimes it's more exciting. Buried treasure. Gold coins or artefacts, which have been lying there under the surface, undisturbed for 2,000 years or so.

Then the woolly archaeologists descend, excavate the field, and set the finds in their historical context. Intriguing. All I get from digging up my garden is an old nail and a painful back.

It starts with just an ordinary field, but there's so much going on under the surface. Translate that into human terms. We're complex creatures, even the simplest of us. And so much lies hidden – our feelings, hopes, beliefs, things we keep well below the surface of life but which make us who we are.

Lord you dig into my life,
unearth my secrets,
and still you welcome me.
That is all I need to know.

Overleaf:
Low Tide, Morecambe Bay, *Watercolour*

"Everyone who drinks this water will be thirsty again,
but whoever drinks the water I give him will never thirst.
Indeed, the water I give him will become in him
a spring of water welling up to eternal life."

I wasn't sure I'd read it right. The words were on a white van belonging to the water supply company. When I got home I checked it out on the Internet. Yes, it was part of their publicity and was in their annual report. The slogan read: 'Your water is safe in our hands.'

My water? I won't venture into the medical aspects of whose and which water they were claiming, but water safe in their hands? I can accept water safe in a reservoir, or even safe in a bucket, but safe in their hands? All my attempts at holding water in my hands come to nothing. It trickles away. Even when I rinse the soap off my face, I have to be quick or the water's gone. And I reckon so will the slogan be when the publicity department reactivates its sense of humour.

I suppose it's just a nice example of people taking themselves a little bit too seriously, but we do need to take care about the way we use language. It's so easy to mean well but for another sense to creep into the words we use without us realising it. And the words come out with the wrong message.

Let's think before we speak, and let's wait a moment before we respond to the things other people say to us. Misunderstanding is so easy – and so difficult to sort out when it's happened. Think twice before we react.

Guard me, Lord, from speaking too much,
too often, and with too little thought.

You will keep in perfect peace him whose mind is steadfast, because he trusts in you.

We'd finished breakfast. Time to get the newspaper, still jammed in the letter-box. In the hall, on the side table, I noticed two envelopes needing stamps. I picked them up, went back into the kitchen, opened the drawer where we keep them. We were down to the last two, so I crossed the kitchen to write it up on the notice board among the things we needed to buy. There wasn't much room – out-of-date notes taking up all the space – so I went to the sink for a damp cloth to wipe the board clean before I wrote down 'stamps'. But where was the felt-tip pen?

The cloth was a bit grey and tatty so I threw it into the waste bin. The bin was nearly full so I took it out to the big wheelie bin in the garage. Then I remembered the felt tip. I'd seen it on the bookcase with Barbara's cookery books, but as I began to look for it I caught a comment on the radio. 'Wonder what it says about that in the newspaper?' I thought. The newspaper? Where's that? It was still in the letter-box. I'll get it as soon as I've finished writing that note about stamps, and found a clean damp cloth and... Oh, well, another busy day. Maybe I should concentrate a bit more, do one job at a time, and if I can find time for God in my day that would make it even better.

Creator Lord, you brought the world
to order out of chaos.
Help me create a little order in my life today.

Ecclesiastes 3:1

There is a time for everything, and a season for every activity under heaven.

Mature people like me – Oh, let's be honest, older people like me – can remember the thrill when the first fresh strawberries of the year appeared, in June or July, depending on the weather. The taste was wonderful, particularly if you'd gone into the fields and picked your own. Hunting the ripest, reddest, juiciest fruit, and then that slightly guilty feeling of clandestinely popping one into your mouth as you picked. Bliss on the taste buds; sweet and slightly acid together.

Yesterday, they were selling strawberries in the greengrocer's. In January. Strawberries in winter. A bit pricey, but tempting in their plastic boxes. Where do they come from? Certainly not local fields. They'll have been flown in or trucked over from Israel or Spain. Or wherever.

But is it such a good idea? When you can get something all the time, whatever the season, the thrill goes. They're not special anymore. There's no excitement – they're just strawberries. In wanting everything, all the time, we lose the rhythm of life. God gives us winter and summer, spring and autumn. Darkness and light. Times of shortage, times of plenty. Waiting for harvest. It's those blank times, when we're just waiting, that makes the fulfilment so full of flavour.

Lord of the seasons, I want to be content with what I have, to take life as it comes and yearn for nothing else but you.

Just as each of us has one body with many members,
and these members do not all have the same function,
so in Christ we who are many form one body,
and each member belongs to all the others.

Driving along the motorway, I was looking for the day's first Eddie Stobart van. That wasn't why I was on the motorway but the Eddie Stobart ritual begins every journey we make. They're everywhere, a nationwide transport group and many folk, just like us, look for them. No, we didn't get the idea from the grandchildren, it just grew. It's somehow comforting, the little detail you can always rely on. Sometimes we have to drive a few miles before we spot one, but we've never been let down yet.

Then, as we drove, I began to notice other vans, other names. One from France, with a name I can't begin to pronounce – my French accent's terrible – then a lorry from Warsaw spelling out a name full of Xs and Zs and almost no vowels, another from Spain, one from Budapest and another from Italy. 'Hope that one's full of red wine,' I thought. Then Prague, and pot plants from Holland.

The whole human family seemed to be driving along the M1. Maybe not quite the whole family, but a large part of it, all before my eyes. Different languages, different cultures, different customs, but all human, just like us, with families at home, and a lifetime of commitment. They're all to be welcomed, even cherished, for the richness they bring to our lives. And if we look really hard, we may just glimpse the image of God in each one.

Lord of surprise, you come to me in many ways
and offer me the joy of finding you in everyone I meet.

Overleaf:
Autumn on Blencathra, Lake District, *Watercolour*

A.D.ASKEW

Finally, all of you, live in harmony with one another;
be sympathetic, love as brothers, be compassionate and humble.

My daily newspaper printed a photo from Iraq. It showed a boy of nine or ten scrambling across a bomb crater, a great hole of broken brick and rubble. The boy looked anxious, and was cradling his pet in his arms – a white rabbit.

The picture moved me more than photos of burning buildings or smoke-filled skies. The boy and his rabbit made it personal. It told me about the way violence disrupts the lives of innocent people, and of their desperate longing to be normal again.

Boys and white rabbits may not be strategically important to the generals, but the picture held a powerful message. It told me that love can survive even through suffering – crystallised here in the love of a small boy for his pet. It was the one living thing he could hold onto, protect, and treasure. It was precious to him.

Not long ago we were celebrating Epiphany, that time of year when churches remember the wise men who followed the star and found Jesus. They came from the East, and probably from the area around Iraq. That was a long time ago, but I hope there may still be a few wise men in Iraq who can spare a thought and some compassion for little people and their unspoken needs. Like the boy and his white rabbit.

Lord of compassion, give me the grace
to open up my life to others' needs.

So God created human beings in his own image,
in the image of God he created them;
male and female he created them.
God saw all that he had made, and it was very good.

Scientists have been comparing the genetic code – DNA – of chimpanzees and humans. We're told they're nearly the same. Estimates vary but they're between 95% and 99% identical. In one sense it's not surprising – every living thing on Planet Earth, animal, vegetable or human, has to use the same basic elements for its make-up.

But if it concerns you to be associated so closely with chimpanzees, I suggest that, looking at the way some human beings behave these days, it should worry the chimps even more to be linked closely with us. And I reckon the most important thing isn't the similarity, but the 5% or 1% difference.

The little extras that make us human. I'm thinking of the good and positive things. The sense of justice that makes us protest at unfairness and inequality. The goodwill that makes people respond so generously when disaster strikes. The love and understanding that motivate so many of our relationships.

We can look at it all negatively when we see some people reverting to the jungle in their behaviour, but the great thing is that goodness survives, and tends to break out when it's most needed.

And if I can find a little gene for that in my make-up, then I'll settle for my closeness to the apes.

Lord of all goodness, I'm only human,
but that is all you want of me;
to walk with you and grow in grace.

> You show that you are a letter from Christ, the result of our ministry, written not with ink but with the Spirit of the living God, not on tablets of stone but on tablets of human hearts.

I was thinking about that science report comparing chimpanzees and humans. Apparently we're very similar in make-up. But the important thing to me is the difference, not the similarity. The little extras that humans have that chimps don't. One is a gene for language, the ability to talk, to communicate with each other.

Here am I, at my computer, writing for people I've never met and sharing thoughts with you – assuming you've actually taken the book off the shelf and started reading that is. Language is one of those precious extras. Apes communicate too, let's not be unfair to them, but not with the depth humans have. And we don't just use spoken words; there's the wonder of writing too.

To think that marks on paper can record facts and feelings, poetry or financial statements, which can be read and understood by people living thousands of miles away. I'm not sure about understanding the financial statements but you see what I mean. And writing can communicate across the centuries. I was reading a book the other day, written 300 years ago, and it still makes sense. And what about the Bible – 2,000 or more years old and still alive and relevant and speaking to us in so many ways.

And thinking of marks on paper – I wonder what marks we shall leave on life today?

Lord, as I make my mark today,
grace it with love and beauty.

...fight the good fight, holding on to faith and a good conscience.

I'd been in Ireland for a week, talking to groups of my readers about the books I write. I'd had no time for painting, and only managed a few very rapid pencil sketches. Frustrating, because Ireland's a beautiful country.

Back home, I thought, 'I must get down to some serious painting.' But I just couldn't begin. My studio was ready – it always is. The easel in its usual place, the paper, paints, brushes all handy. Yet I made every excuse I could think of not to start. Do the shopping, tidy the greenhouse, check and reply to my e-mails, write a thought for the day – anything to put off the painting.

Eventually I ran out of excuses. I opened my sketchbook, took a deep breath and began. Three bad paintings later – they all went into the waste paper basket – I paused. 'Maybe I should wait until I feel more like it?' I thought. 'Maybe I should wait for inspiration?' But it doesn't work like that. If you wait for the inspiration, you'll never begin. It's another excuse. You just have to pick up your brush, mutter a prayer and get on with it. The inspiration, as we call it, comes through the striving and the mistakes. And, yes, the fourth painting was passable, my inhibitions have gone, and I'm back on course.

Many of the best paintings seem effortless but that comes out of the struggle. I reckon that's how character is formed. Whether we paint or not, and whatever today may bring, it's going to be a challenge.

*Lord, when the battle's hardest
I need the courage and the
confidence that only you can
give, to stand and start
again each time I fail.*

Overleaf:
Golden Days, *Watercolour*

Jeremiah 29:11

"For I know the plans I have for you," declares the Lord,
"plans to prosper you and not to harm you,
plans to give you hope and a future."

"You can have those photos," said Joy. "They're your family anyway." Joy and David are new friends and we went round to spend an evening with them. When we arrived, Joy brought out a battered Victorian photo album. She turned a few pages and there was my granddad. A little label identified him, but I recognised the face from other photos I have.

As a little boy, I remember him telling me stories of army life in India, but now here he was, in the uniform of a World War I army officer – a lieutenant, resplendent in riding breeches, Sam Brown belt, swagger stick and gloves. Then other photos – my dad as a six-year-old with his brother and sister, and later as a teenager. Three generations back, Joy's grandfather and mine had been good friends, and three generations later so were we.

I remember finding an album of Victorian family photos in an antiquarian book shop. They'd been brought in by someone who'd inherited them but had no interest in his family history. How sad, but maybe his hadn't been a happy family. His photos weren't of much financial value but they could have given him a sense of belonging, as my family pictures do for me.

The photos of my granddad help me to know a little more about where I've come from: but maybe it's even more important to know where I'm going.

Lord of today, just take my hand and
bring me safely home.

*But a Samaritan, as he travelled, came where the man was;
and when he saw him, he took pity on him.*

Life's gone a bit pear-shaped recently. My wife, Barbara, has been taken ill and had several weeks in Queen's Medical Centre in Nottingham. It started with an early morning 999 call. The ambulance rolled up – and soon she was blanketed, strapped in safely and on her way to hospital.

The paramedics were superb. Both men, really competent and very gentle. Reassuring too, all the way to Accident and Emergency. Then the organisation took over. Decisions all in other people's hands; people we didn't know, had never met before. We were no longer in charge of our own lives. We were fed into the system.

What impressed me most though, amid all the cool professionalism, was one paramedic. He was one of the two in the ambulance who'd answered our emergency call and delivered us to hospital. About an hour later we were into all the tests and admission procedure when he walked back in, just to see how my wife was getting on. That was great. It wasn't part of his job to care like that, but he was concerned for her, and perhaps a little for me.

In the tension and anxiety of the morning, I didn't remember his name. It was just one of those quiet acts of kindness that helped the day along. I hope someone shows him this page. I'd like to say thank you.

---

*Lord, I thank you for the kindness of strangers.
May I recognise your presence in their lives.*

---

*"Come to me, all you who are weary and burdened,
and I will give you rest."*

Driving along the other day, I saw something on the road. Just a tatty plastic shopping bag. Too many of them around, I thought. As I drove over it – no, I couldn't stop to tidy it up, there were other cars behind me – the wind whipped it up into the air. The last I saw of it, in the rear-view mirror, it was dancing in the slipstream of my car. It swirled high, then down and sideways like a manic seagull, until the following car caught it and started the process all over again. The bag was off once more, whipped along by forces it couldn't control.

I've been feeling a bit like that since Barbara, my wife, has been in hospital. Events have been happening beyond my control. I've had to rely on other people – doctors, nurses, physiotherapists – and never been quite sure what would happen next. Far from sorting things out myself, the way I like to do, other people have been in control both of Barbara's life and mine.

Blown around like that plastic bag, I seemed helpless and not a lot of use, but the feeling doesn't last. First, I thank God there are others to take control when I'm out of my depth – the professionals. Then, there are the friends who step in and lighten the burden, and say those words that mean so much, "We're thinking of you, and praying for you." That's great.

Lord of uncertainty,
when I am pushed around
and don't know where to turn,
help me to trust you with my worries.

I wait for the LORD, my soul waits, and in his word I put my hope.

Queen's Medical Centre, F floor. I was waiting for a lift to take me down to the main entrance on B. I'm past walking down the stairs for four floors even if the alternative is to wait. There are three lifts on every landing but, when I press the little button on the wall, the lifts are usually well down at ground level. All you can do is stand and stare at the three closed doors, and wait. Then, like the proverbial buses, two lifts come together.

Sometimes, wherever we are, all we can do is wait. We may feel we need to move on from where we are, but doors seem to be firmly shut. However hard we wish to change things, we just have to wait. It's out of our hands. Waiting's often harder than doing, but we don't get anywhere banging on the wall or repeatedly ringing the bell. The lift will come when it's good and ready, and bring with it new opportunities. Maybe the waiting time's been given to encourage us to think things through a bit more carefully.

And when the lift finally arrives, we have a choice. Ignore it, or step into it, press a button, and hope it'll take us where we want to go. Life's a bit like that.

Lord of time and eternity, stand with me when the waiting's hard,
and teach me patience. But do it gently please.

Overleaf:
Frosty Morning, *Watercolour*

"I have told you these things, so that in me you may have peace.
In this world you will have trouble.
But take heart! I have overcome the world."

While Barbara was in hospital recently, she lost her wristwatch. It was only a cheap Timex. I'd bought it for her so that she could leave her good watch at home. Just as well, or she'd have lost the good one. I asked around, nursing staff, cleaners, no one had seen it. Not in the bathroom or under her pillow, nowhere. "Ah well," I thought, "It's no big deal." Illness tends to put things into a different perspective.

Back home, I opened the washing machine – amazing how domesticated I'm getting – and started to unload all the clothes I'd brought home from the hospital. As I took out the last towel, I heard something rattle. I looked into the machine, felt around with my hand, and there was Barbara's watch. I'm not quite sure how it got there. I think she'd put it into a pocket and forgotten, and I hadn't gone through the pockets before putting the clothes in the washer.

Anyway, there it was. A bit of the strap was frayed, the plastic cover slightly scratched, but it still told the time. Totally immersed in hot water and soap, spun at 1400 revs per minute, it still worked. Something I needed to take to heart. Barbara's been going through the mill with her stroke but, hopefully, when we've worked through all the struggle and anxiety, she'll come out at the other end, maybe more careworn than she was, but still in working order. And that will be because of all the TLC – tender, loving care – she's getting, even though at times it feels like going through the wringer. But then, Jesus knew all about that.

Lord of life, it's not easy, I confess, to live
the peace you offer, but with your help
I'll make it through another day.

Right:
Geese, *Watercolour*

The Lord is the stronghold of my life – of whom shall I be afraid?

I bought a pair of geese a while ago. Not the living, feathery sort; these were bronze sculptures. I'd been looking for something to be a feature in the garden and I spotted one outside a shop which sold custom-made kitchens. No, don't ask the connection.

I went to look at the goose. The man said he had another inside, a different pose. We haggled for a moment or two on the price – a haggle of geese rather than a gaggle? – and we brought them home. We've arranged them on the patio around an old sundial. They look great and very much at home.

A little complication though. At the time we had a very old dog. He'd had a long and active life but now he couldn't walk far or see very well. He spent most of his time asleep, but from time to time he would visit the garden. The first time he got near enough to the geese to see them, he stopped, looked, and began to bark. He felt threatened. He barked again, and when the geese didn't move he edged forward, and finally had a puzzled sniff. It happened a few times over the next couple of days and then he accepted them.

It's easy to stand and bark when we're confronted with something – or someone – we don't recognise or understand. We feel threatened. Much better to take a look, move forward, maybe even take a sniff, and come to terms with it – or them. And, as time goes on, we may even welcome the new and let it enrich us.

Lord, I see so many things to bark at in my world.
Help me to welcome and accept the new
and different with grace.

**Do not condemn and you will not be condemned.
Forgive and you will be forgiven.**

Our youngest grand-daughter, Georgia, is six-going-on-25. Talking to Mummy the other day, Georgia asked, "Mum, can we run time backwards?" What a question from a six-year-old. Mum probed a bit. No, Georgia hadn't been watching sci-fi films on telly. She'd been with a group of school friends sharing sweets, and Georgia had missed out. There hadn't been enough to go round. She thought if she could go back in time and live that bit over again, she could make sure she got a sweet.

Running time backwards. I guess we'd all like to do that at some time in our lives. To savour some happy moment, or to get a chance to put right something we regretted. "If only I had my time over again, I'd do that differently," we say.

The trouble is we can't turn the clock back, or run time in reverse. We simply – or not so simply – have to try to get it right first time. That's not always possible – I know that well from my own experience, but there can be comfort in looking honestly at mistakes we've made, facing the consequences and saying sorry. And when it's the other way round and someone's upset us, comfort in forgiving them.

And if we could run time backwards and get another chance, who's to say we'd get it right the second time round?

---

*Forgiving Lord, I offer you my failures and regrets.
Knowing that I've tried my best
must be enough for me right now.*

Matthew 6:34

"Therefore do not worry about tomorrow, for tomorrow will worry about itself. Each day has enough trouble of its own."

Milli, the new puppy, is black and brown and beautiful, and she seems to know it. She's full of life. I'd taken her out into the garden and was watching her rooting around near the pond. I was standing near the long, glass, sliding doors that open out onto our patio.

Suddenly there was a blur of movement, a rush of wind past my head, a tangle of feathers and a powerful thud. A large bird had misinterpreted the glass and flown at full speed into the window. It lay on the ground, twitched a couple of times, and lay still. I waited a few moments in the hope that the bird was just stunned, then picked it up gently, but there was nothing I could do. That was it.

I looked at the sleek bouncing beauty of Milli, full of energy and life. Then I looked again at the bird in my hand, still beautiful but lifeless. It put a shadow on my day. Life's a mixture for all of us. Joy and sadness, good and not-so-good, hope and disappointment. These ups and downs are all part of the great cycle of living that we share and belong to. It's all part of being human and we can't seal ourselves off from it, or live in a vacuum. And, in a strange way, it makes us what we are, adds to our perspective on life and, just perhaps, adds a little wisdom.

And Milli's still here, adding to the joy of life.

Lord of life, help me to live it well today,
and when the edges of my understanding
get a little frayed, strengthen my faith.

Overleaf:
Colours of Autumn, *Watercolour*

But the fruit of the Spirit is love, joy, peace, patience, kindness, goodness, faithfulness, gentleness and self-control.

Did you know that dogs like watching television? Well, Milli, our new puppy, certainly does. Yes, she really does. She's not very selective and can't use the remote control yet, but she knows what she likes. Rather, she knows what she doesn't like. She doesn't like other dogs on the box. The moment she sees one, or hears one bark, she's there, growling at the screen. She doesn't realise the dogs aren't real – just virtual images as we say – she barks anyway.

We used to have a dog who disliked opera singers, particularly tenors. Whether it was Placido Domingo, or Pavarotti or Carreras, it was all the same to him. When he heard them sing, he sat in front of the telly, head in the air, and howled.

But back to Milli. It's not only dogs. Anything large that moves quickly across the screen disturbs her. She just doesn't understand that the threat isn't real, there's no danger. I know people like Milli. People who feel threatened by anything or anyone new or different. And whatever they don't understand they do the human equivalent of barking at it. Even if there's no real threat.

But if I look honestly at myself, I'll find I sometimes do the same. But it's better to be positive, to welcome the new and the different, and to think twice before we bark. Or even learn not to bark at all. That's our next job in training Milli.

You ask a lot, Lord. Where shall I start?
Maybe with patience –
I guess that's where
you have to start with me.

*For in this hope we were saved. But hope that is seen is
no hope at all. Who hopes for what he already has?
But if we hope for what we do not yet have,
we wait for it patiently.*

Our dog, Milli, has had a friend staying with us – Toby, our daughter's dog. Milli's small and black. He's large, black and hairy. They get on well together but at feeding time we keep them at a distance. We put Milli's food in its usual place, but Toby's at the other end of our fairly large kitchen. The separation's important. Toby could eat for England in the Dog Olympics and come back with a medal. It takes him about eight seconds to hoover up everything in his bowl and then he looks over towards Milli. She's slower and has only just finished sniffing her food and deciding which bit she'll eat first, when he saunters over in her direction. He's not aggressive; he just hangs around in case anything gets left over.

The funny thing is that when Milli's finished her food she does the same thing in reverse – goes over to Toby's bowl on the off-chance he's left something. Neither dog ever leaves a crumb, but they're hopeful that this time it'll be different. It never is but they live and hope.

Or should it be hope and live? I was interviewed recently for a magazine article. I was asked, "When you were ten years old, what did you want to be when you were grown up?" "Alive," I answered. We can't really live without hope can we? Whether we live in Nottingham or West Sudan, it's only hope that keeps us going.

Lord of my future, I can do the hope,
but patience wears a little thin at times.
I need the help that only you can give.

"Peace I leave with you; my peace I give you."

We've just put Jesus back in his old cardboard box and returned him to the loft. He'll be safe enough there, with Mary and Joseph, and the shepherd with his sheep. The three wise men are with him too, in case he needs some advice. Oh, and an angel.

We dusted Jesus down for Christmas and put him out with the other pottery figures on a side table in the hall. I don't know what he made of the sprigs of holly with their thorny leaves, or the ribbons decorating the table. There were lots of folk – family and friends – coming and going, so he had plenty of opportunity to share his goodwill and peace on earth. For us that was a bit of a strain at times, but we did our best.

But now, he's safely back in his box in the loft, along with the goodwill and peace on earth, and we can go back to being our usual critical selves again. A bit of a relief for most of us. There are some folk though who believe that the peace and goodwill are meant to go on in our lives right through the year, but that's too much to expect. Isn't it?

Lord, if I sometimes box you in,
bang on the lid until I let you out into my life again.

"Freely you have received, freely give."

Time to renew my motor insurance. Same time every year. Do I look for a new insurer, or stick with the old? Everyone seems to want my business. Adverts everywhere saying, "We're cheaper than the others. Save money with us."

I had this idea. If I went to an insurer who said he was cheaper and got a quote, I could mention that to the next insurer and get one cheaper still. Then on to the next and, if I worked at it, I'd get insurance cover for nothing. And, in my deepest fantasy, someone might even pay me for joining them.

The trouble is it doesn't happen like that. Something for nothing never works out that way. Not just in motor insurance but in relationships too. Relationships cost. They cost in commitment; we can change our motor insurance every year but if we try that in our relationships we're soon in trouble. They cost in effort too. In caring for the other person. It doesn't come cheap but in our relationships the more we give the more we get in return, although that's not why we do it. It's all about that four-letter word: love.

Generous Lord, nothing comes for nothing,
except your love. Thank you.

Overleaf:
Harvest Fields, Norfolk, *Watercolour*

A.D. ASKEW

Taking the five loaves and the two fish and
looking up to heaven, he gave thanks and broke them.

The postman brought a parcel of books this morning – not unusual in our house. There were three copies of a book of graces – the little prayers some folk say when they sit down to a family meal together. A small thank you for the food.

The editor of the book had invited a number of people, including me, to write a new grace, or contribute one from the past. There's a wide range from all over the world. One thing I noticed was a greater gratitude for food in the prayers from Africa, where food isn't taken for granted the way it is in the West. There are prayers from many communities, Christian, Hindu, Muslim, Sikh – after all, we all share the same need for food – and graces that remember the hungry wherever they are.

Not so many of us say grace these days but it's still worthwhile. Whatever our religious faith or none, it's still good to acknowledge our dependence on others for the food we eat. There just has to be someone to thank.

Whether that's God, or the efforts of the farmer who grew the food, the sailors who transported it, or the cook who put the food on the table, we can say thank you. And it's worth remembering that the food on the table is the result of someone else's hard work and often sacrifice. So whether it's just a quick cup of coffee on the move, or cornflakes and toast, or a full English breakfast, say thank you, out loud or in your heart. Now.

Lord of the harvest,
thank you.

"What are mere mortals that you are mindful of them, human beings that you care for them? You made them a little lower than the angels; you crowned them with glory and honour and put everything under their feet."

Members of The Spotted Dog Art Group spent a day painting in my garden. Why Spotted Dog? Well, the first committee was trying to think of a name that people would remember. As they were talking, the door pushed open and in walked Spot, the hostess's dog. The Spotted Dog Art Group it was, although Spot's not learnt to paint yet. It's a group with a good mix of talent, from hesitant beginner to confident painter, and all willing to share their experience.

Anyway, a group came, minus Spot, to paint in my garden. The garden looked colourful, the weather was great, and we had a productive time. It was interesting to see the individual paintings. One painter chose a wide-angle view, others did more close-up studies. All were different, from broad-brush to detailed. Some in watercolour, others in pastel or pencil.

Whatever the subject or style, what excited me was the shared creativity. And, whatever the level of skill, each person was creating something unique, making marks on paper that no one had ever made before. Creativity makes humans different from other living creatures – the imagination to see a picture in our minds and put it down on paper. The same with writing and music. It's a divine gift, a sharing – in a tiny way – in the pool of creativity we call God.

We're only human, but our humanity's a many splendoured thing, and there's a little bit of God's creativity in everyone of us.

Lord of the imagination, spark me into life,
to see the beauty in your world and,
if I can, inspire me to add a little beauty of my own.

Good people bring good things out of the good stored up in their heart...

I went into a large showroom the other day. It wasn't very busy but the receptionist was sitting at her desk. She greeted me with a warm smile. 'That's nice,' I thought, 'you don't always get that.'
"How are you today?" she asked.
"Fine," I answered, "and how are you?"
So far, so normal.

"I'm very well," she said, then paused and added, "and I'm very happy." Unusual.
"Why's that?" I asked, intrigued.
"Because I love my job."
"That's great," I said. "Tell me more."

She said that in her last job she'd found it difficult to get up on Monday mornings and start another week. In this job she was always happy to come. I asked what made the difference. What made her happy here? She said it was the people – the customers. They were all so nice. I asked her about the staff, her colleagues. Yes, them too.

I thought about it. Customers, and workers, come in many shapes and sizes, they can't all be perfect. I reckoned there was more to it than that. I believe it was her own attitude that created the happiness. Her openness, that same friendliness she'd shown me, her willingness to help.

And her expectations. She was positive, looking for good in the people she met, and because she was looking for good, she found it. She was creating good feeling and that can be infectious. God bless her, she made my day.

Lord of all joy,
let me see the good in those I meet today.
And if it's hard to find,
to dig a little deeper till I do.

---

1 Thessalonians
5:16-18

Be joyful always; pray continually; give thanks in all circumstances, for this is God's will for you in Christ Jesus.

Why are the lights always at red? I was driving into Nottingham the other day, and at the village crossroads the lights said stop. Then a right turn onto the main road and 200 yards along there's a pedestrian crossing. Red again. Next crossroads – can you guess? Yes, red once more. So it went on all the way to the park-and-ride.

As I sat on the bus and let the driver take the strain I asked myself, "Why are the lights always at red?" The answer of course is that they're not. I'm sure there are times when they're all at green and I drive through them happily, accepting them without thinking. The greens just don't register. But when they're at red, it's different, and I complain.

When things go wrong, when life's at red, it leaves a mark on us. I protest; wish things were different. But when my life's at green and everything's fine, I hardly notice it. Just take it for granted when really I should be thankful.

So next time the lights are green, accept it as a gift for the day. And, when they're at red, just remember the good days you've known. And incidentally, when the lights show red it's usually for our safety – and the safety of others.

And the amber? Well, it could go either way. Take care, but say yes to life.

"Give thanks in all circumstances"?
That's a tough one, Lord,
but with your help I'll make a start.
It won't be easy, but I'll try.

Overleaf:
Winter Farmstead, *Watercolour*

Psalm 111:4

He has caused his wonders to be remembered;
the LORD is gracious and compassionate.

The snow took us by surprise. It was only the middle of November. Earlier in the day, men had been around our road sweeping those multicoloured autumn leaves into great piles of gold, struggling against a very mischievous wind. I've sometimes thought it would be more convenient if each tree had just one big leaf. Then, when it fell, we could fold it up neatly and dump it on the compost heap. Quick, convenient, neat. Anyway – a bit later a large truck arrived and vacuumed the leaves away. All that random beauty consumed, tidied away, finished.

Then the snow came, its fall turned to gold by the evening street lights. Next morning, looking out of the kitchen window into our garden, I saw one solitary rose still blooming. A beautiful apricot pink, standing out against the bleakness of a cold winter's day. Not protesting, just standing there, being a rose. One small flower, insignificant – no, not insignificant, because in the bleakness it gave my heart a lift.

A splash of colour, and beauty, and joy to start the day. Perhaps, if I'd gone up close, even a hint of fragrance. Don't give up, it seemed to say, don't let the gloom take control. There's new life around the corner. Fix it in your mind and keep going. J. M. Barrie, the author of the Peter Pan story, wrote 'God gave us memory so that we might have roses in December.' Even in November the words make good sense.

Lord of surprises,
when life seems cold and bleak,
colour my day with joy.

Galatians 6:2

Carry each other's burdens, and in this way
you will fulfil the law of Christ.

We were having a late family holiday in the Lake District. We enjoy going out of season in the colder weather. There's something special about the landscape when the trees have dropped their leaves. We were walking, my wife Barbara, two daughters and husbands, and four grandchildren.

Georgia, the youngest, is a good walker, very determined, and rarely complains. But after a succession of rough paths she was tired. "Carry me, Daddy" and up she went on his shoulders. I wished he could have done the same for me - paths seem to get steeper these days – and my knees aren't what they used to be.

We all need a carry at times. Not literally, I'd look a fool perched on my son-in-law's back. But now and then, particularly in winter, life can seem to stand still and we feel we're living in a monochrome, monotonous world. That's when we need the encouragement of a friend, a sympathetic listener. Someone who'll help carry us along. And the best way to find one? By giving someone else the lift and encouragement they need today. Then maybe, when the lights go to red in your life, there'll be someone around to share your feelings and give you the support you need.

Lord, sometimes my burdens seem too heavy
and my energy too light.
But if you'll take the other end,
I'll try to lift my share.

Be completely humble and gentle;
be patient, bearing with one another in love.

Our little dog, Milli, protects us from harm. That's her view, anyway. We have a fairly big garden and every morning she rushes out to check it. The other day, the early morning quiet was shattered. Milli was barking frantically. I rushed out to quieten her. We have good neighbours but I wasn't sure how they'd enjoy being woken up at a quarter past six.

There was Milli, running from side to side like a collie herding sheep. But it wasn't sheep, it was a fox. Milli had it cornered. I think that the fox could really have made a meal of Milli, but it just stood there with its back to the hedge. My sudden appearance changed the balance. It couldn't stand the two of us and with a graceful leap the fox found a hole in the hedge and was off.

And Milli? A last growl and she came to tell me how tough she was. I wasn't quite as sure as Milli. I don't think confrontation is always the best way to deal with a crisis. There are other, quieter ways of defending our personal territory. And, if we try, we can usually accommodate the other person, even if they have a different opinion from ours. It's worth the effort anyway. And, who knows, maybe they're right.

Lord, if I could only think before I growl,
listen before I shout, see the good
and offer space and dignity to those with whom I disagree.

The Leprosy Mission

Restoring health, hope and dignity

The profits from the sale of this book are going to the work of The Leprosy Mission in hospitals and rehabilitation centres in the developing world.

Leprosy is a medical condition affecting millions of people, 90% of whom live in the developing world.Leprosy causes disability and even blindness, if untreated, by attacking nerves under the skin, leading to loss of feeling, paralysis and unfelt injury of the hands, feet and face.

Leprosy is completely curable with Multidrug Therapy (MDT) in as little as six months. Around 3 million people are currently affected by Leprosy and every year between 200,000 and 400,000 new cases are found around the world – over 800 people every day. Fear of the disease often causes rejection and exclusion from one's home and community and can often do more damage than the disease itself. Approximately 12% of new cases found by TLM are already suffering some form of irreversible disability or deformity. TLM programmes deliver a combination of compassion and action. While we do identify and assist people to a cure and treat physical impairments through reconstructive surgery we also invest in education, vocational training, counselling and socio-economic rehabilitation.

TLM Trading Limited, the trading arm of The Leprosy Mission, sells a range of gifts, greeting cards, books and audio. Our work helps raise vital funds for The Leprosy Mission and helps raise awareness of The Leprosy Mission and its work. We also sells products made directly by leprosy affected people, helping them to create sustainable and dignified livelihoods.

If you would like information about...
• Our mail order gift catalogue
• The Leprosy Mission's work
• Prayer support
• Supporting The Leprosy Mission financially
• Service overseas with The Leprosy Mission
• Making and amending a will and leaving a legacy to TLM

Contact us on...
Tel: 0845 166 2253 (local rate, UK only) Email: enquiries@tlmtrading.com

Shop online at www.tlmtrading.com
To purchase one of Eddie's paintings,
visit www.eddieaskew.co.uk

Index of
Bible references

Index of
Bible references

Autumn Road, *Gouache*

Eddie and Barbara Askew joined The Leprosy Mission in 1950. After 15 years serving in India, they transferred to London where Eddie became International Director of the Mission's worldwide operations. Eddie retired in 1987 and was then able to devote more time to his love of writing and painting. When he died in 2007, he had written 17 bestselling Christian books. We will always be grateful to him for his dedication and leadership and we will never forget his compassion, creativity and great sense of humour.

OTHER BOOKS WRITTEN AND ILLUSTRATED BY EDDIE ASKEW

A SILENCE AND A SHOUTING
Eddie's first compilation of 32 Bible readings, prayers and meditations.

DISGUISES OF LOVE
Eddie explores the disguises of love revealed through the pain and suffering of Christ.

MANY VOICES ONE VOICE
31 prayers and meditations that help us to listen out for God's voice amidst the daily clamour of life.

NO STRANGE LAND
'There is no strange land to God. His love, compassion and healing are at work wherever we are.'

FACING THE STORM
A book that encourages us to hang on to our faith while we wait for the storm to pass.

BREAKING THE RULES
When Jesus broke the rules of Jewish society, he demonstrated that the essence of life is not in law but in loving.

CROSS PURPOSES
Eddie shows us that 'The purpose of Jesus' cross is to cancel out the cross purposes of the world.'

SLOWER THAN BUTTERFLIES
Life is fast these days; Eddie invites us to step aside for a few moments each day and pause for thought.

MUSIC ON THE WIND
Eddie encourages us to hear the music of God's love as he takes us through the life of David.

EDGE OF DAYLIGHT
Eddie's fascinating memoirs of his life with TLM, notably his 15 years as a missionary in India and his later travels across the world as TLM's International Director.

TALKING WITH HEDGEHOGS
35 *Thoughts for the Day* that encourage us to think about how we influence our own lives and those of the people around us.

UNEXPECTED JOURNEYS
Readers are challenged to examine five familiar Bible stories and to consider the journey each character makes.

LOVE IS A WILD BIRD
'Love is a wild bird... Give it the freedom to fly and, if it returns, it's truly yours.' One of many inspiring thoughts in this splendid collection.

ENCOUNTERS
Five characters encounter Jesus face-to-face and their lives are wonderfully transformed.

BREAKING THROUGH
Eddie guides us through five Bible stories in which Jesus breaks through the conventions, reaching out to people of different cultures.

ALL OF THESE BOOKS CAN BE BOUGHT FROM TLM TRADING LIMITED
Telephone 0845 166 2253 or shop online at www.tlmtrading.com